Guitar Chord Book

By Peter Pickow.

Exclusive Distributors:
Music Sales Corporation
257 Park Avenue South, New York, NY10010, USA
Music Sales Limited
14-15 Berners Street, London W1T 3LJ, UK.
Music Sales Pty Limited
20 Resolution Drive, Caringbah, NSW 2229, Australia.

©Copyright 1983 by Amsco Publications

Contents

How to use this book

The Guitar Case Chord Book is unlike any other chord dictionary you've seen. It's different in the way it's organized. The result is a completely new kind of reference book that's easier to use and more instructive, whether you're looking up an unfamiliar chord, or checking out a new form for a chord that you already know. The book is tailored to fit right into your instrument case too, so you can always have it on hand when you're most likely to need it.

The Guitar Case Chord Book groups chords in a new way that makes looking up and learning new chords easier for you. The chords are grouped by family, so the chords you're likely to find together in any one piece are next to each other in the book. You can understand how they are related at a glance.

For example, if you look under the heading Key of C, you'll find all the different C chords listed there–C, CM7, C6, C7 and so on. But you'll also find the *related* chords as well, like Am, Dm, Em, F and G. Since every major key shares chords with its related minor key, the major and minor keys overlap. In the same way, if you look under the heading Key of A Minor, you'll find all the different Am chords listed there as expected. But you'll also find the related chords for the key of C as well.

Chord diagrams in the *Guitar Case Chord Book* also indicate the position of the root, and the position of the third. Both moveable and non-moveable chords are included. In case you aren't familiar with the diagrams in the book, here is what they represent:

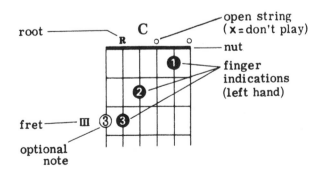

C

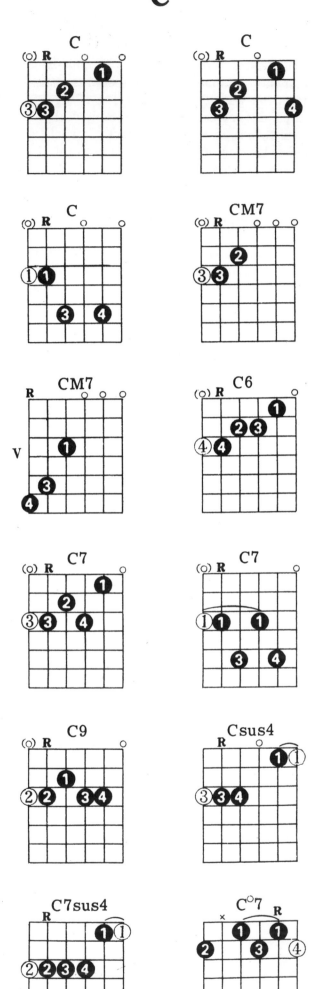

C
continued

Dm
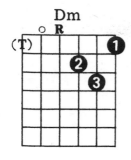

Dm7
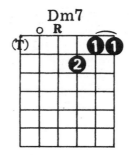

Em
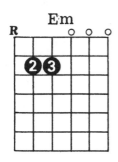

Em7
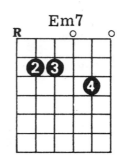

F
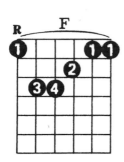

FM7
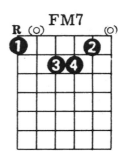

FM7
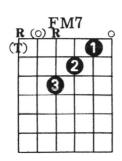

F6
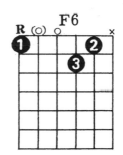

G
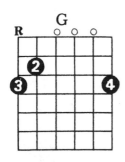

G7
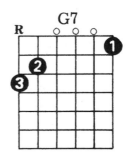

G7
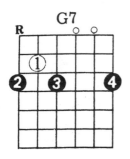

G9
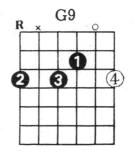

For songs in the key of

Am

Am
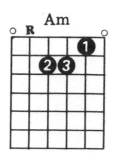

Am
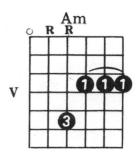

Am7
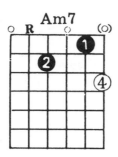

Am7
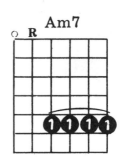

Am6
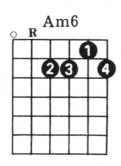

Am6
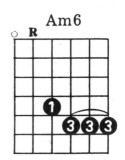

E
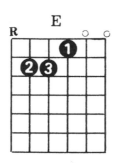

E7
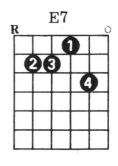

E7
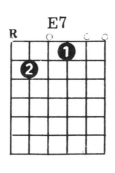

E7
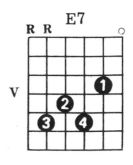

E9
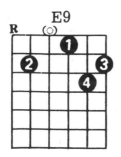

E9
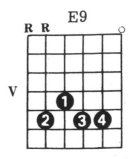

For songs in the key of
G

G

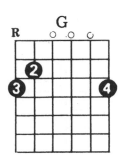

G

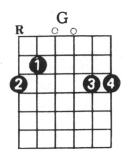

GM7

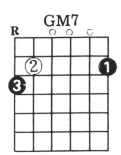

G6

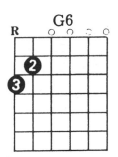

G6

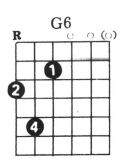

G7

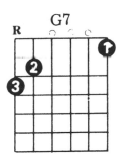

G7

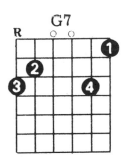

G7

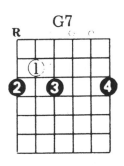

G9

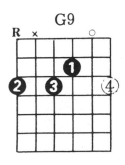

Gsus4

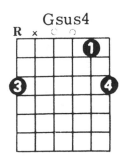

G7sus4

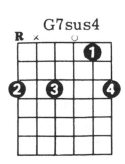

G°7

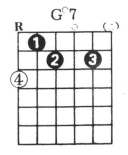

continued overleaf

G
continued

Am

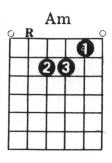

Am7

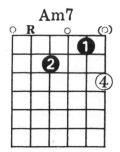

Bm

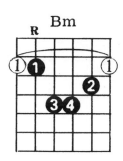

Bm7

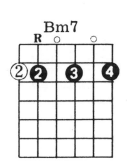

C

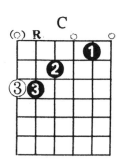

CM7

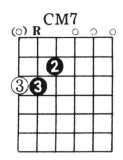

C6

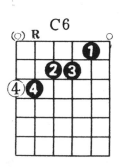

D

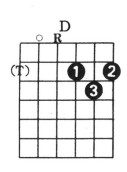

D7

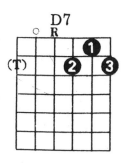

D7

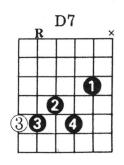

D9

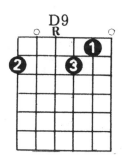

D9

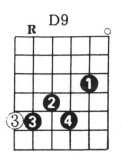

For songs in the key of

Em

Em

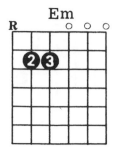

Em

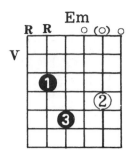

Em7

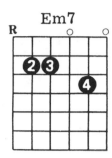

Em7

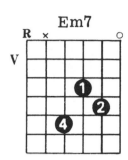

Em7

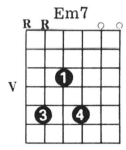

Em6

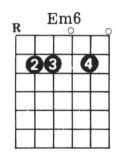

Em6

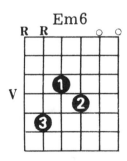

B7

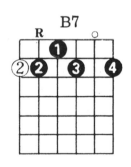

B9

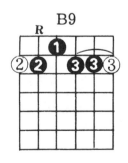

B9

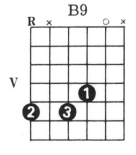

For songs in the key of

D

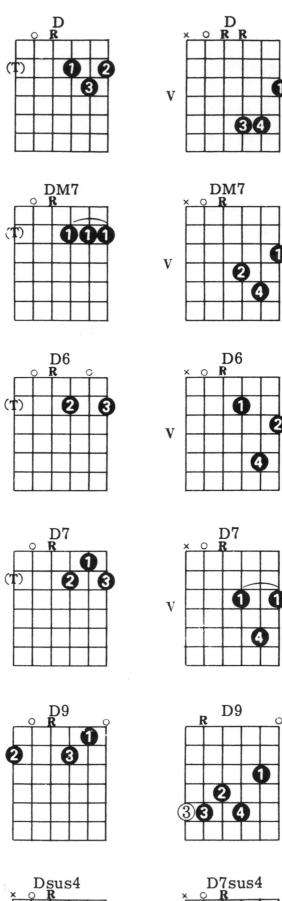

10

D
continued

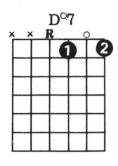

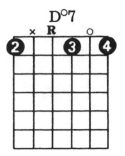

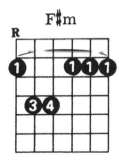

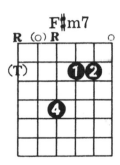

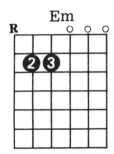

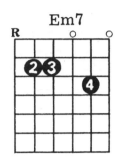

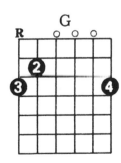

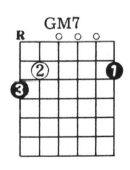

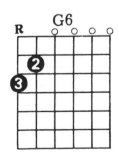

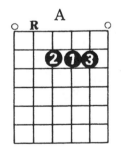

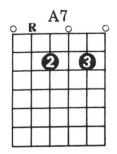

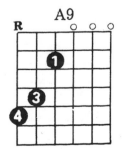

11

For songs in the key of

Bm

Bm
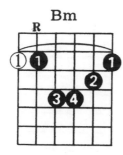

Bm
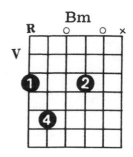

Bm7
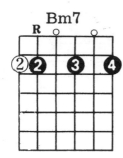

Bm7
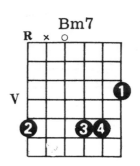

Bm6
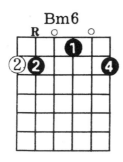

Bm6
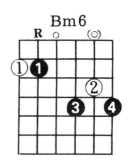

F♯
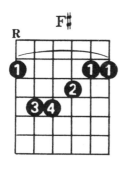

F♯7
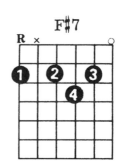

F♯7
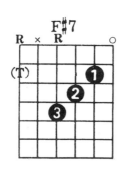

F♯9
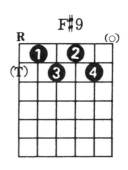

F♯9
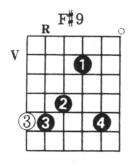

F♯9
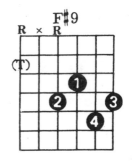

12

For songs in the key of

A

A

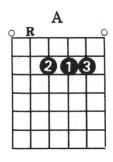

A

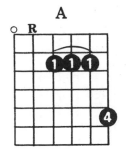

A

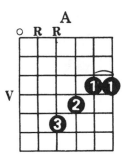

AM7

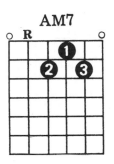

AM7

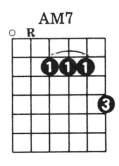

AM7

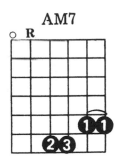

A6

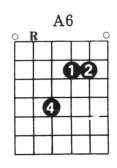

A6

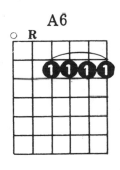

A6

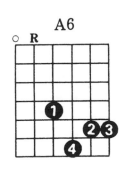

A7

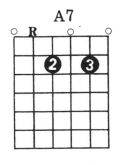

A7

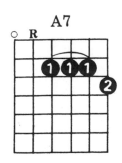

A7

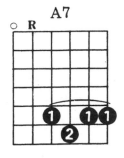

13

continued overleaf

A
continued

A9
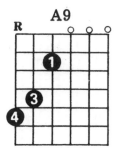

A9
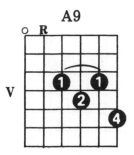

A9
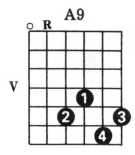

Asus4
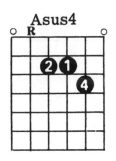

Asus4
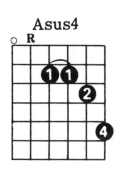

Asus4
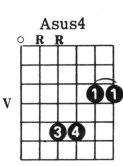

A7sus4
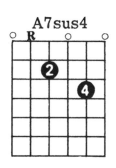

A7sus4
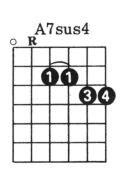

A7sus4
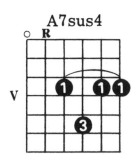

A°7
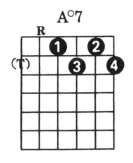

Bm
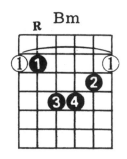

Bm7
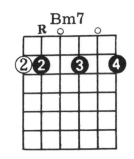

14

C#m
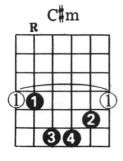

C#m7
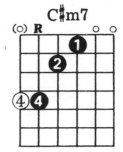

D
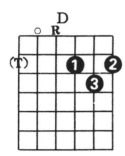

DM7
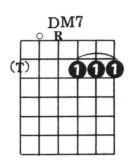

D6
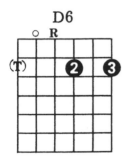

E
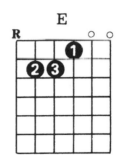

E7
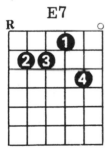

E9
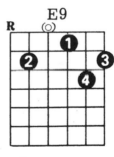

For songs in the key of

F#m

F#m
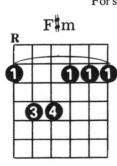

F#m7
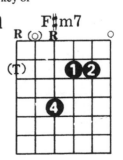

F#m6
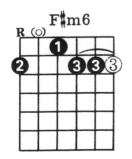

C#
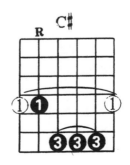

15

continued overleaf

F#m
continued

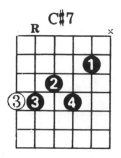

C#7

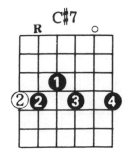

C#7

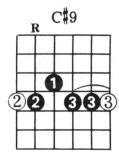

C#9

For songs in the key of

E

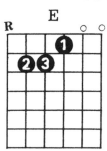

E

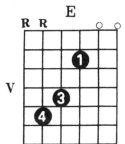

E

V

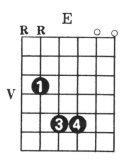

E

V

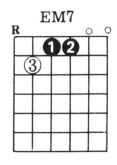

EM7

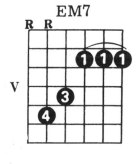

EM7

V

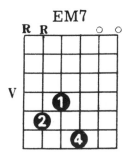

EM7

V

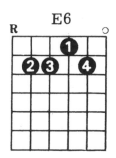

E6

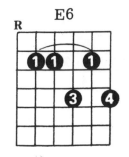

E6

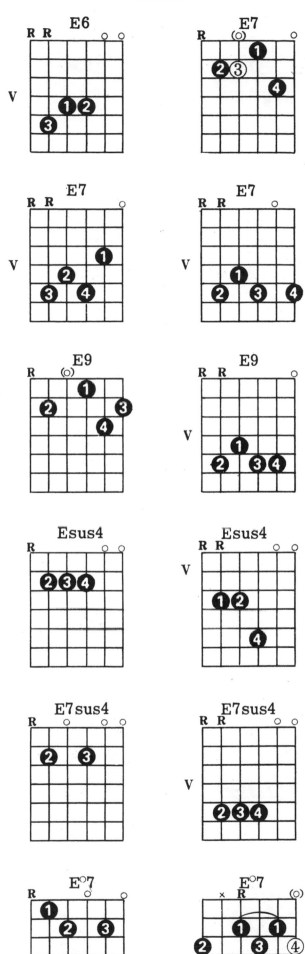

continued overleaf

E
continued

F#m

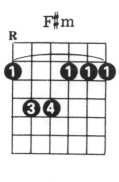

F#m7

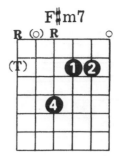

G#m

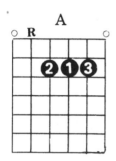

G#m7

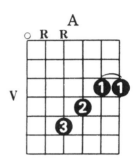

A

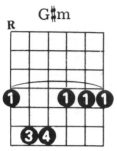

A

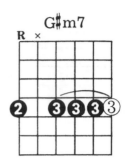

AM7

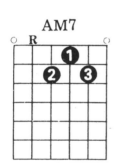

A6

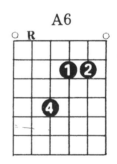

B

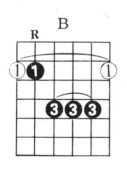

B7

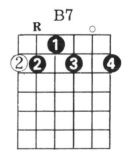

B9

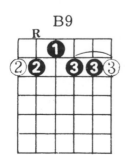

B9

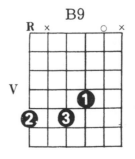

18

For songs in the key of
C#m

C#m
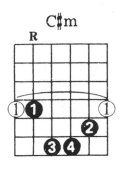

C#m7
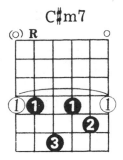

C#m7
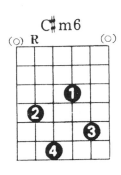

C#m7
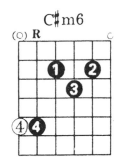

C#m6
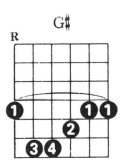

C#m6
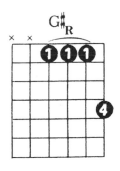

G#
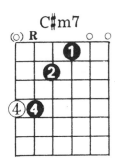

G#
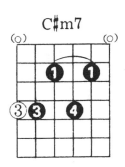

G#7
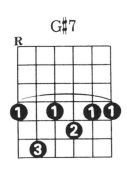

G#7
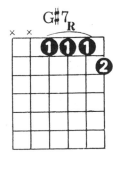

G#9
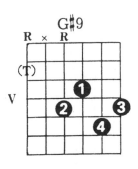

G#9
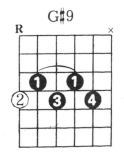

For songs in the key of

B

B

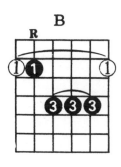

BM7

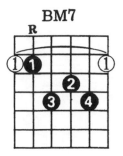

B6

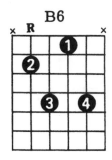

B7

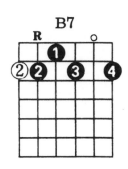

B9

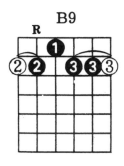

B9

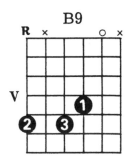

Bsus4

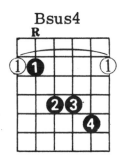

B7sus4

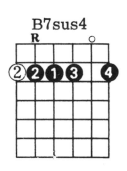

B7sus4

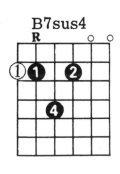

C♯m

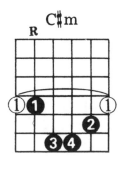

C♯m7

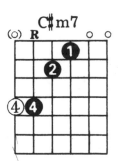

D♯m

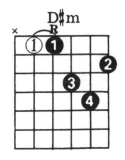

20

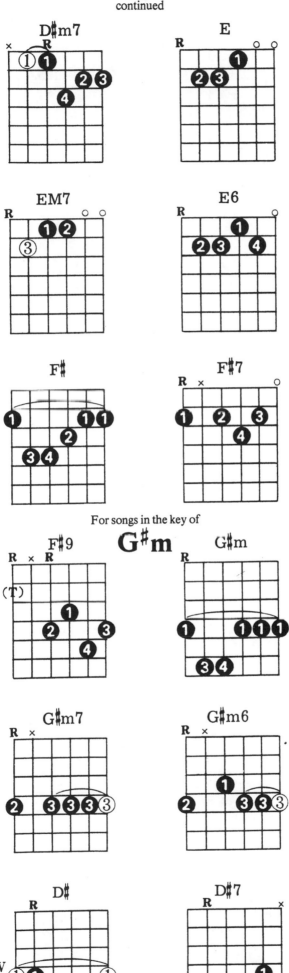

For songs in the key of

G♯m

For songs in the key of
G♭

Gb
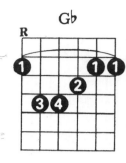

GbM7
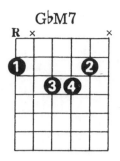

Gb6
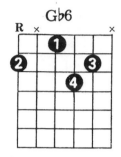

Gb7
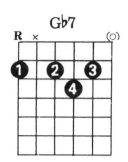

Gb7
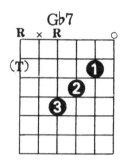

Gb9
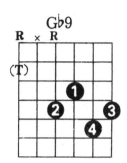

Gbsus4
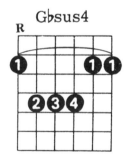

Gb7sus4
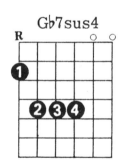

Abm
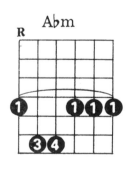

Abm7
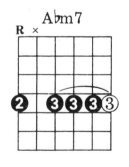

Bbm
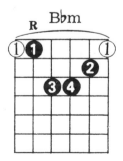

Bbm7
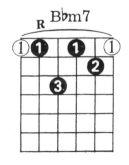

22

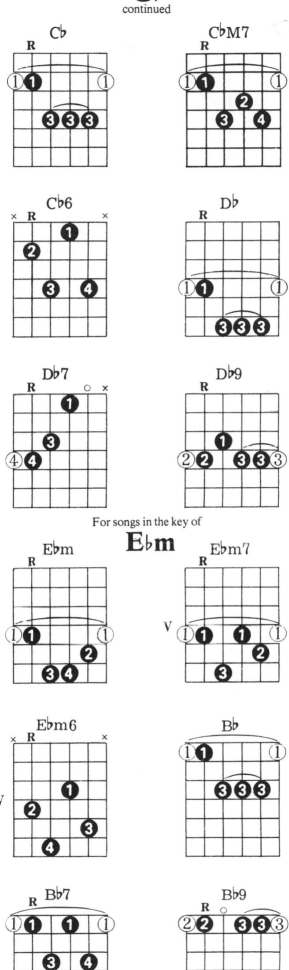

For songs in the key of
E♭m

For songs in the key of
D♭

D♭
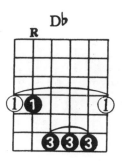

D♭M7
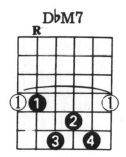

D♭6
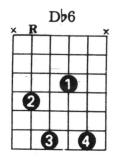

D♭7
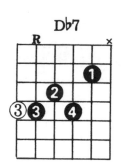

D♭7
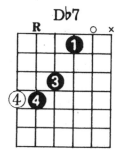

D♭9
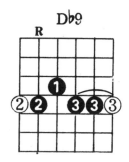

E♭m
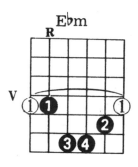

E♭m7
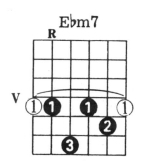

Fm
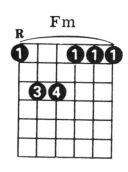

Fm7
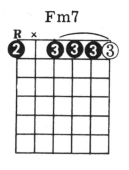

G♭
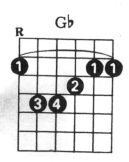

G♭M7
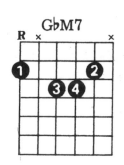

24

D♭
continued

G♭6
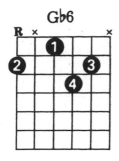

A♭
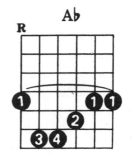

A♭
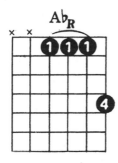

A♭7
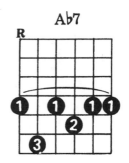

A♭7
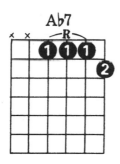

A♭9
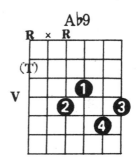

For songs in the key of
B♭m

B♭m
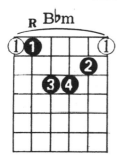

B♭m7
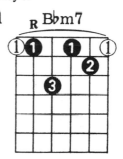

B♭m6
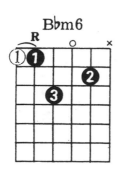

B♭m6
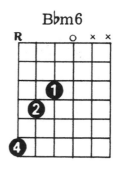

F
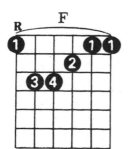

F7
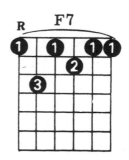

continued overleaf

B♭m
continued

F7

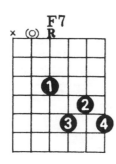

F9

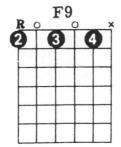

F9

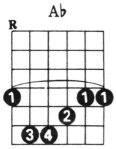

For songs in the key of

A♭

A♭

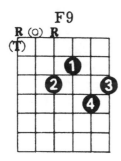

A♭

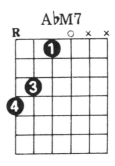

A♭M7

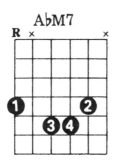

A♭M7

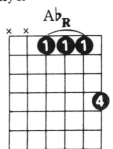

A♭M7

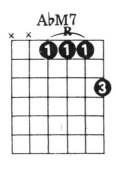

A♭6

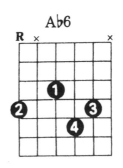

A♭6

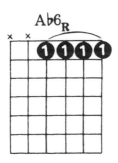

A♭sus4

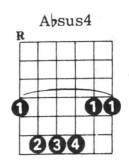

26

A♭
continued

A♭7sus4
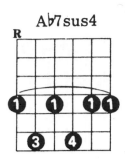

A♭7sus4
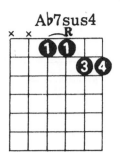

B♭m
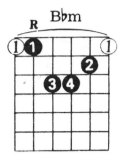

B♭m7
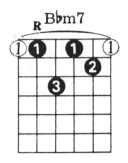

Cm
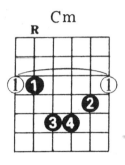

Cm7
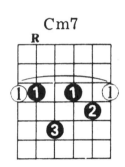

D♭
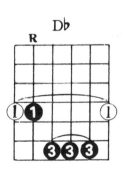

D♭M7
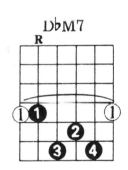

D♭6
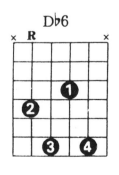

E♭
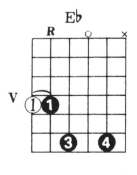

E♭
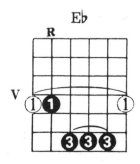

E♭7
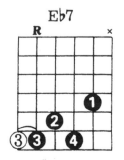

27

continued overleaf

A♭
continued

For songs in the key of
Fm

E♭9
R

Fm
R

Fm7
R ×

Fm6
R × ○

C
(○) **R**

C7
(○) **R**

C9
(○) **R**

For songs in the key of
E♭

E♭
R ○ ×

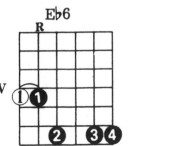

E♭6
R

E♭7
R ×

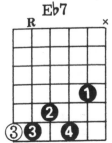

28

E♭
continued

E♭9
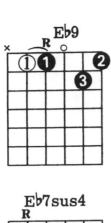

E♭sus4
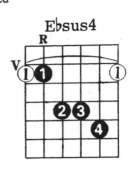

E♭7sus4
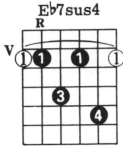

Fm
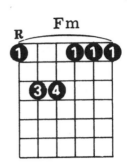

Fm7
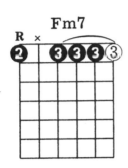

Gm
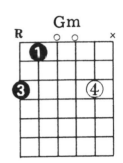

Gm7
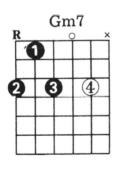

A♭
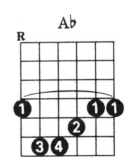

A♭M7
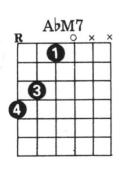

A♭6
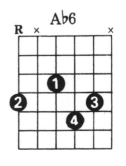

B♭
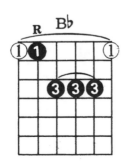

B♭7
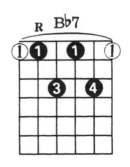

29

For songs in the key of
Cm

Cm
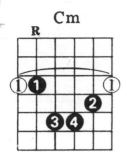

Cm
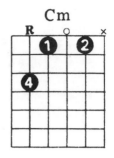

Cm
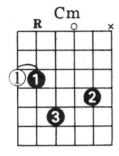

Cm7
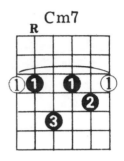

Cm6
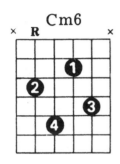

Cm6
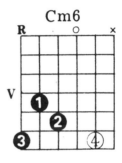

G
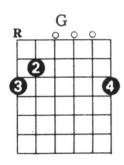

G7
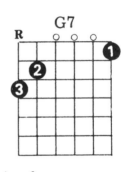

G9
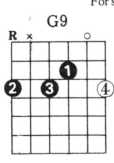

For songs in the key of
B♭

B♭
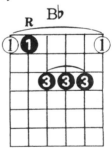

B♭M7
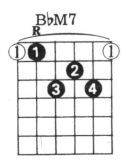

B♭6
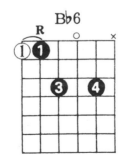

B♭
continued

B♭6
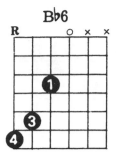

B♭7
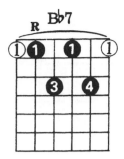

B♭9
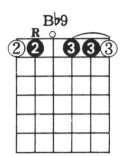

B♭sus4
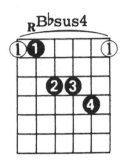

B♭7sus4
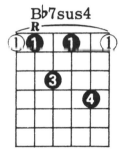

Cm
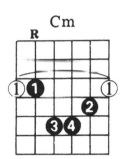

Cm7
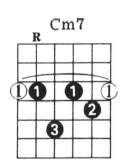

Dm
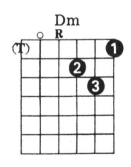

Dm7
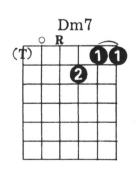

E♭
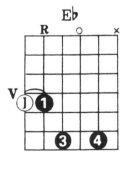

E♭M7
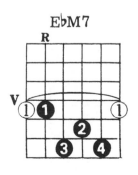

E♭6
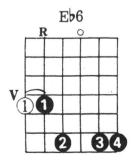

31

continued overleaf

B♭

continued

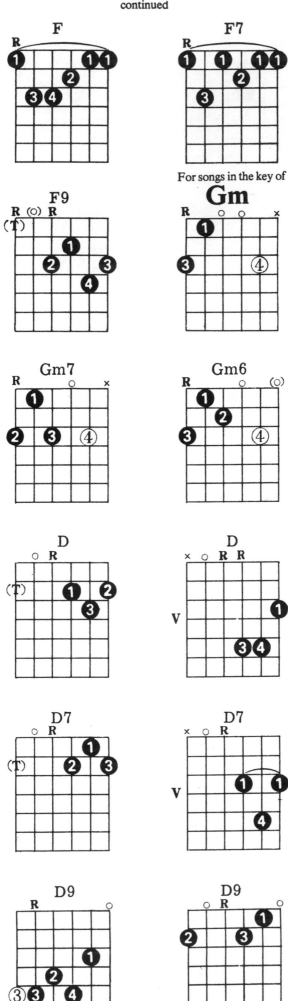

32

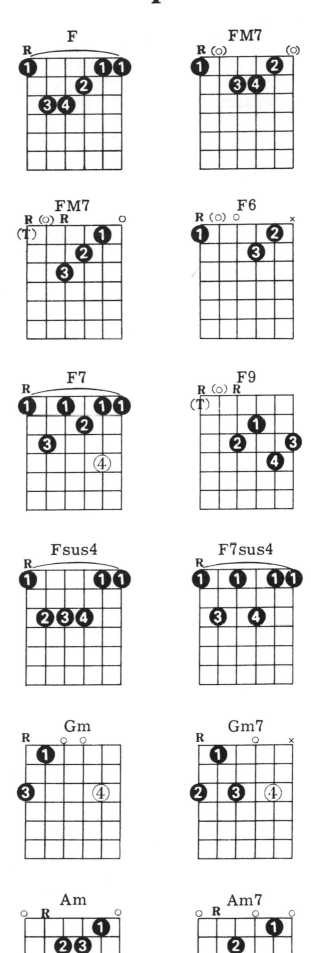

continued overleaf

F
continued

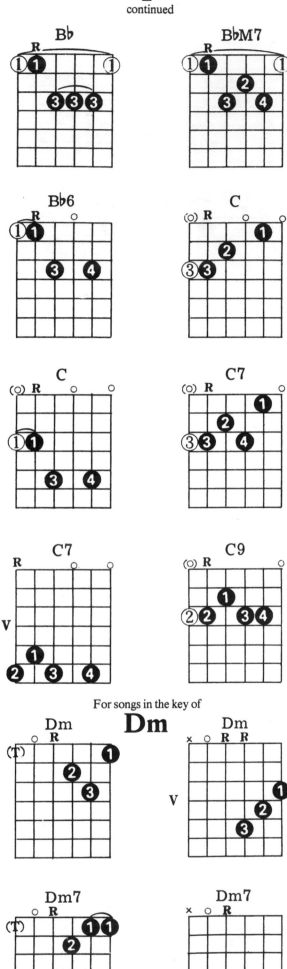

Bb

BbM7

Bb6

C

C

C7

C7

C9

For songs in the key of
Dm

Dm

Dm

Dm

Dm7

Dm7

Dm
continued

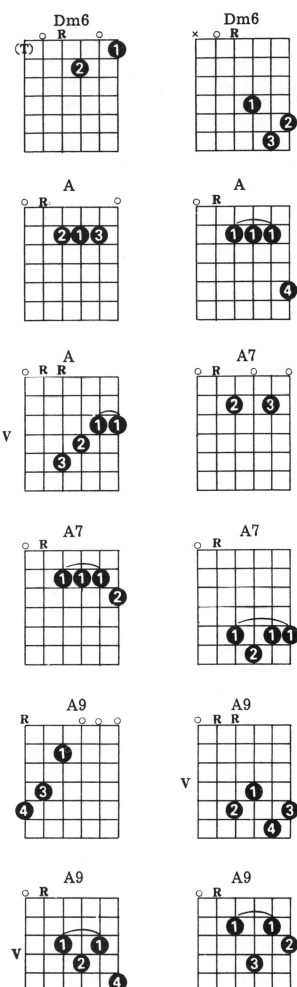

Moveable chords (Major)

Root on sixth string

M
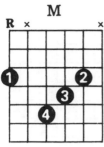

M7
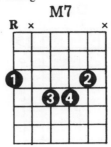

7
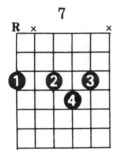

6
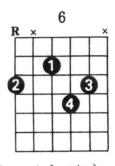

Root on fifth string (fifth on sixth string)

M
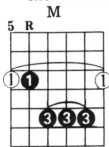

M7
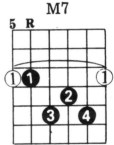

7
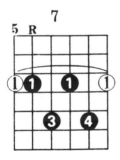

6
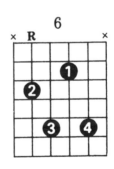

Root on fourth string (fifth on fifth string)

M
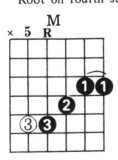

M7
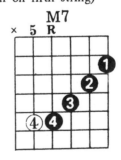

7
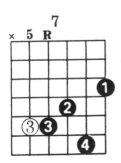

6
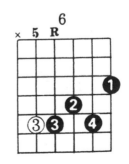

Moveable chords (minor)

Root on **sixth** string

m
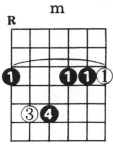

m(M7)
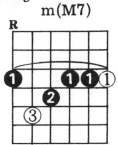

m7
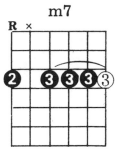

m6
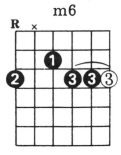

Root on fifth string (fifth on sixth string)

m
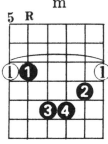

m(M7)
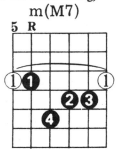

m7
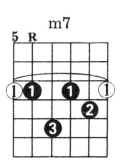

m6
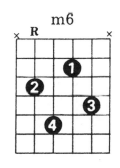

Root on fourth string (fifth on fifth string)

m
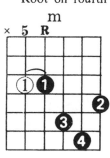

m(M7)
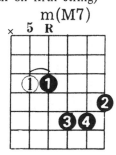

m7
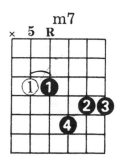

m6
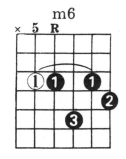

Inversions (Major)

Third on sixth string

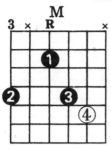

M

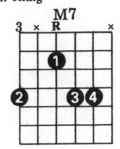

M7

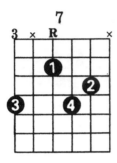

7

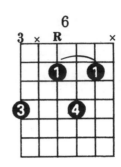

6

Third on fifth string

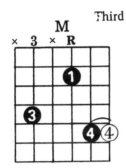

M

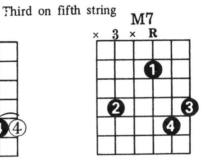

M7

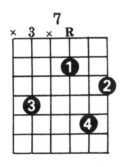

7

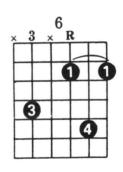

6

Third on fourth string

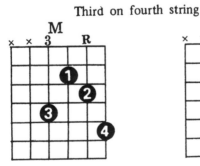

M   M7

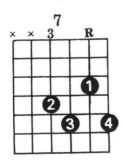

7

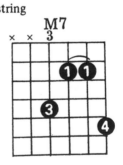

6

(minor)

Third on sixth string

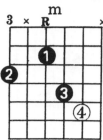

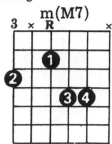

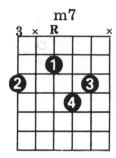

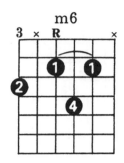

Third on fifth string

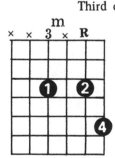

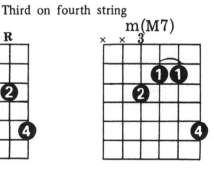

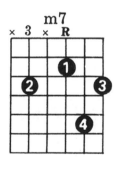

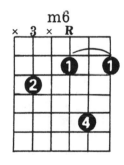

Third on fourth string

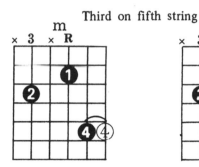

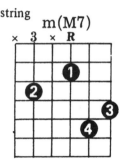

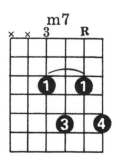

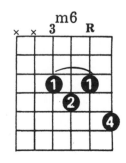

(Major)

Fifth on sixth string

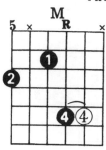

M

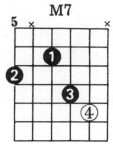

M7

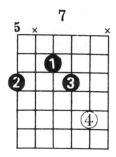

7

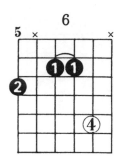

6

(minor)

Fifth on sixth string

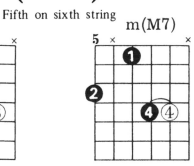

m

m(M7)

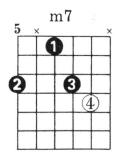

m7

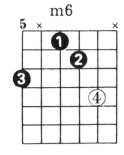

m6

Miscellaneous moveable chords (Major)

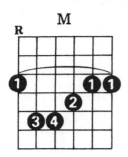 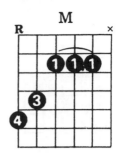

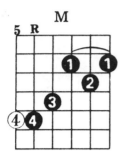 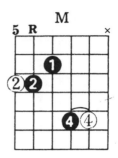

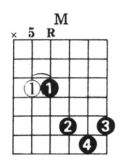 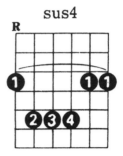

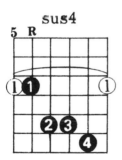 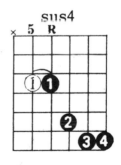

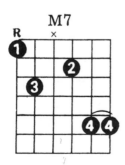 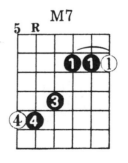

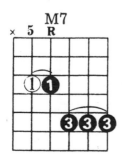 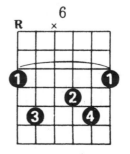

41

continued overleaf

6

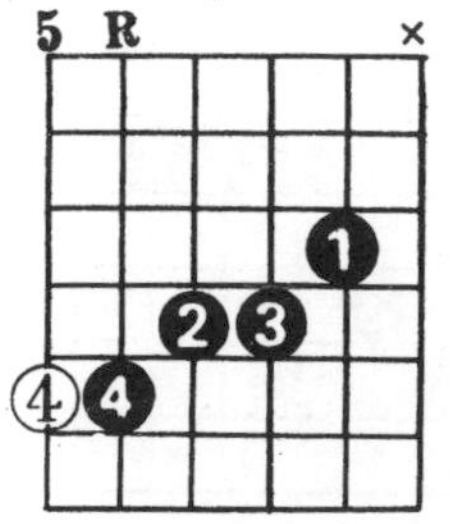

6

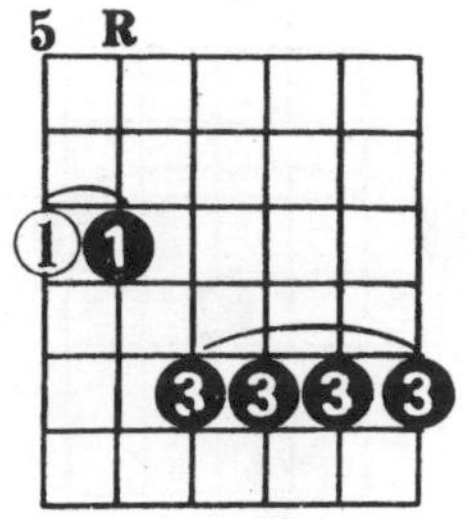

6

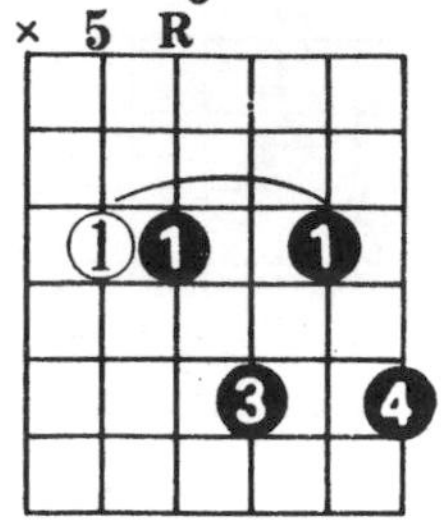

6
9

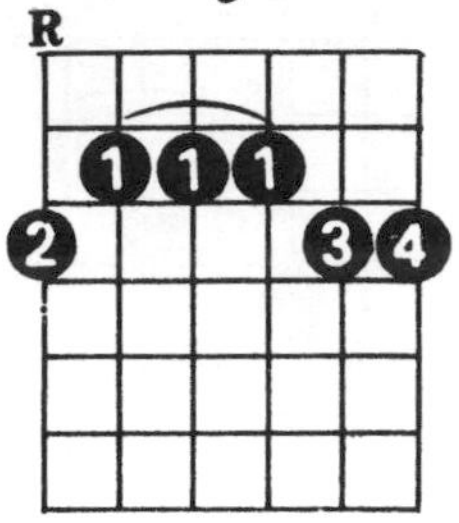

6
9

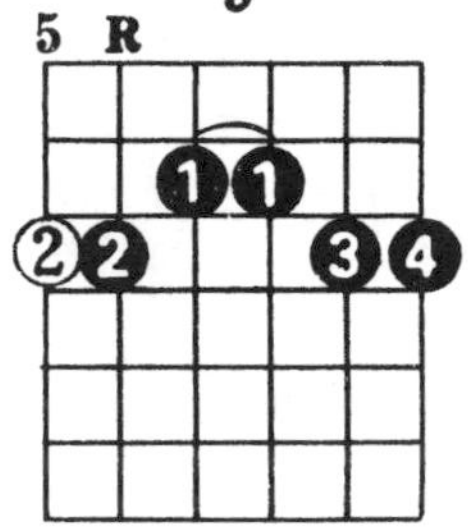

M9

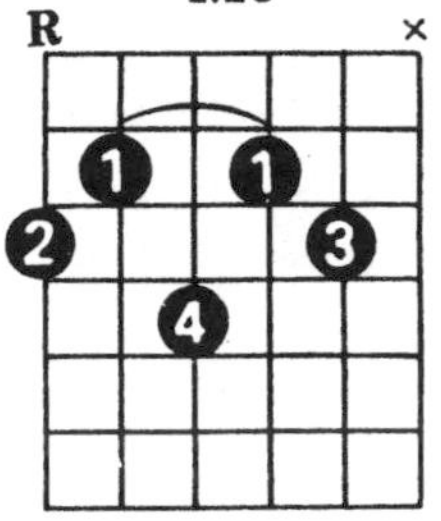

M9

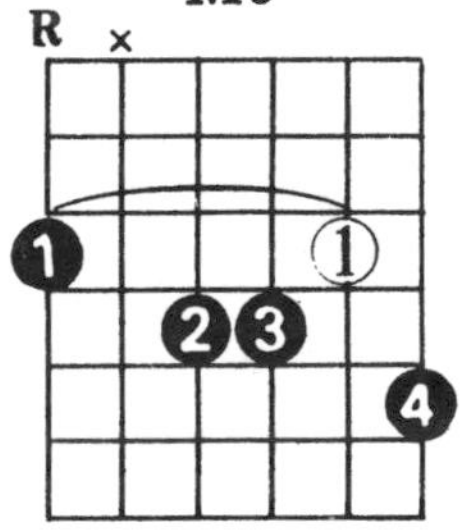

M9

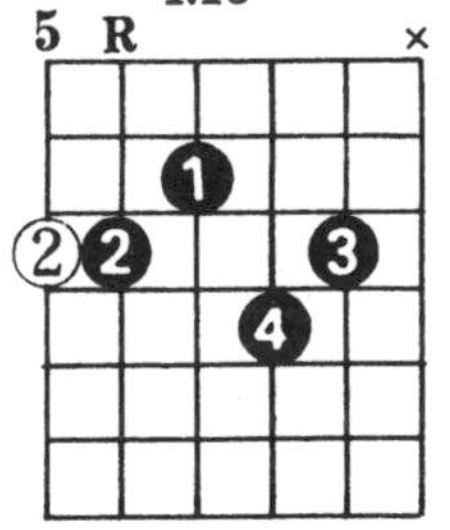

M13

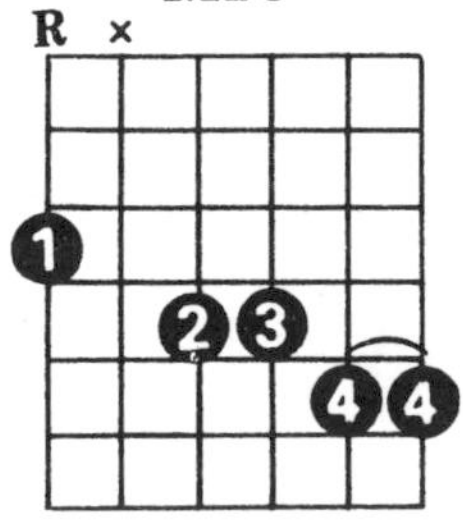

M13

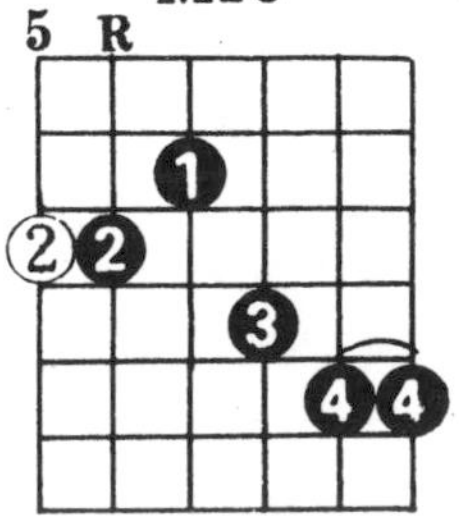

7

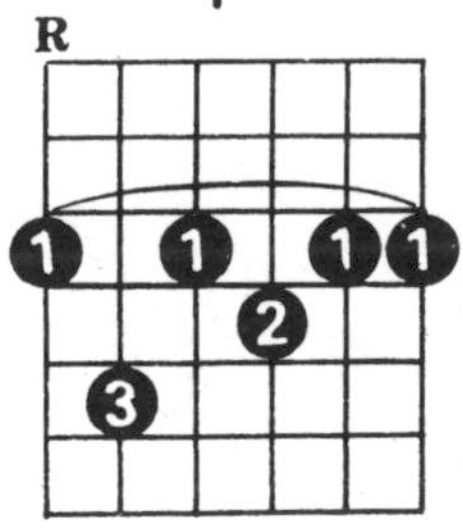

7

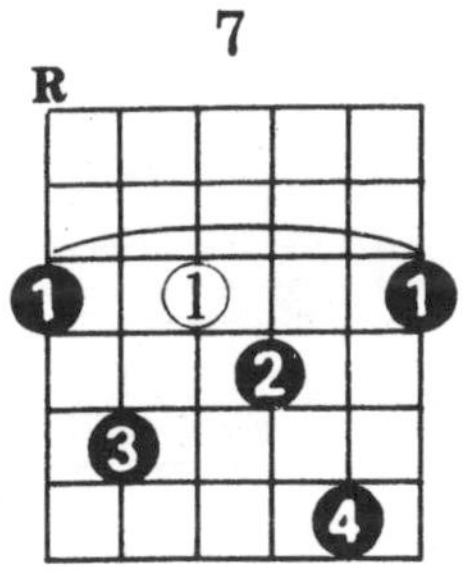

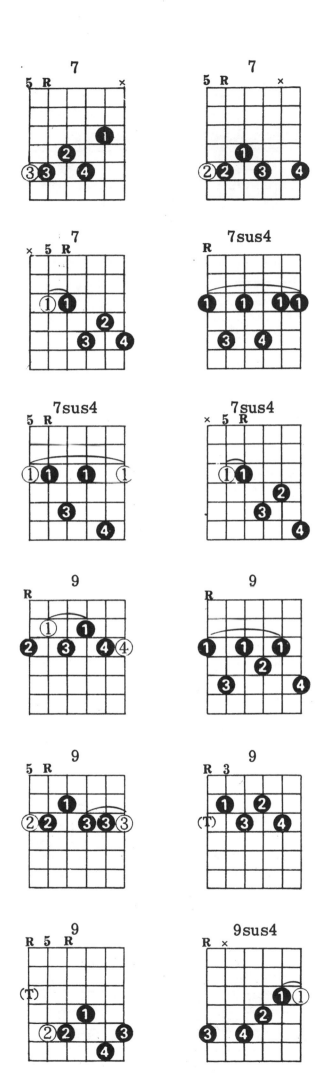

continued overleaf

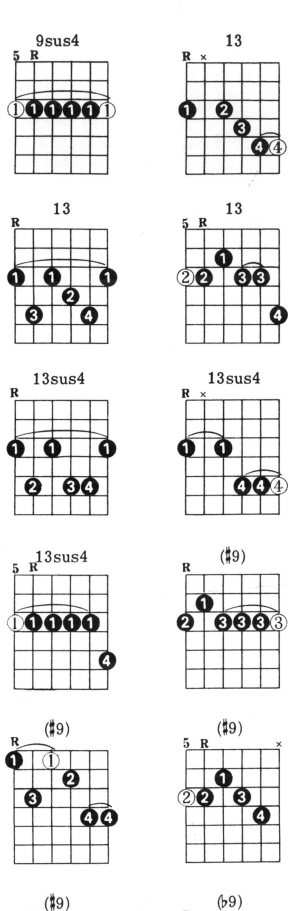
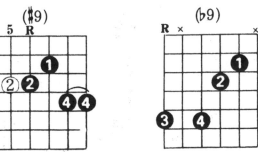

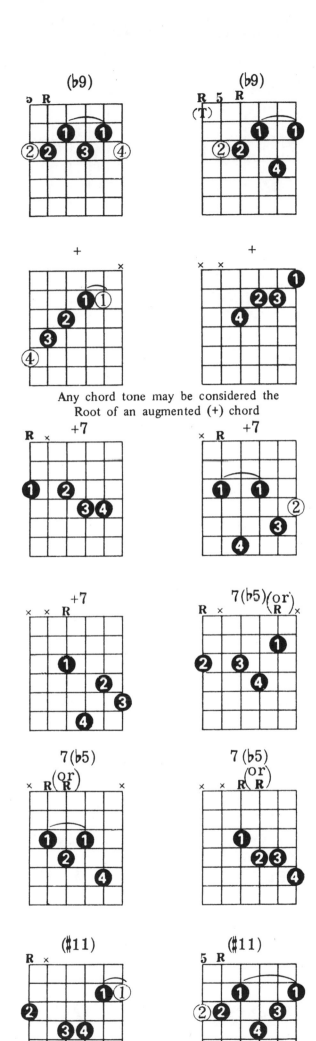

Any chord tone may be considered the
Root of an augmented (+) chord

Miscellaneous moveable chords (minor)

m
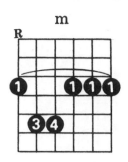

m
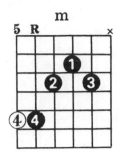

m(M7)
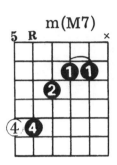

m7
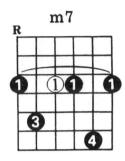

m7
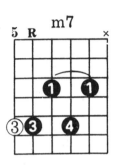

m7
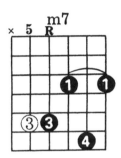

m6
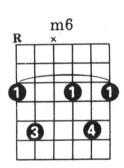

m6
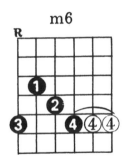

m6
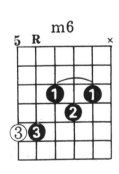

m6
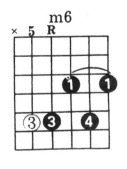

m9
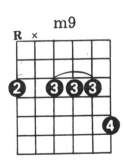

m9
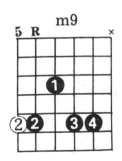

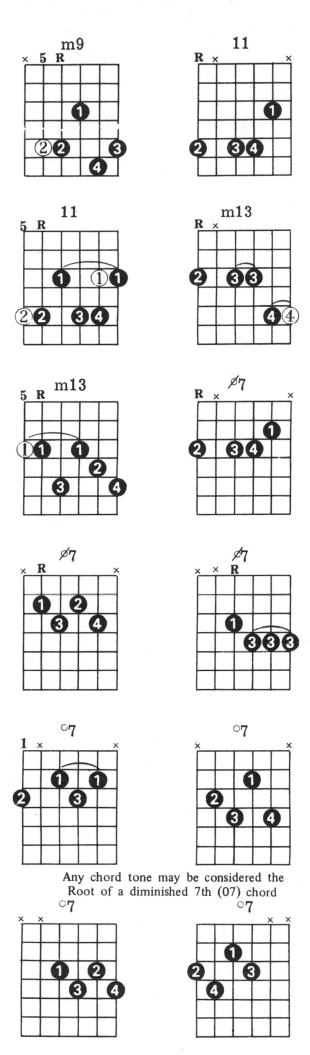

Any chord tone may be considered the Root of a diminished 7th (07) chord

Common chord symbols found in music books

and how to locate them in this book.

Symbols used in this book	Name	Alternate Symbols
M	Major	Maj
m	minor	min; –
6	Major Sixth	Maj6; M6
m6	minor sixth	min6; –6
$\frac{6}{9}$	six-nine	6(add9); Maj6(add9); M6(add9)
M7	Major seventh	Maj7; △
7	dominant seventh	
m7	minor seventh	min7; –7
m(M7)	minor with Major seventh	min(Maj7); m(+7); –(M7); min(add M7)
$^{\varnothing}7$	half-diminished seventh	½dim; ½dim7; m7(♭5) m7(–5)
$^{0}7$	diminished seventh	0; dim; dim7
+7	augmented seventh	7+; 7(♯5); 7(+5)
7(♭5)	dominant seventh with flat(ted) fifth	7(–5)
9	dominant ninth	7(add9)
M9	Major ninth	△ (add9); Maj7(add9); M7(add9)
(♭9)	dominant flat(ted) ninth	7(♭9); 7(add ♭9); 7–9; –9
11	minor eleventh	min11; m11; min7(add11); m7(add11);
(♯11)	Major (or sharped) eleventh	(+11); △(+11); M7(+11); △(♯11); M7(♯11)
13	dominant thirteenth	7(add13); 7(add6)
M13	Major thirteenth	△ (add13); Maj7(add13); M7(add13); M7(add6)
m13	minor thirteenth	–13; min7(add13); m7(add13); –7(add13); m7(add6)
sus4	suspended fourth	(sus4)
+	augmented	aug; (♯5); +5

Chart of enharmonic equivalents

A♯ = B♭

B = C♭

B♯ = C

C♯ = D♭

D♯ = E♭

E = F♭

E♯ = F

F♯ = G♭

G♯ = A♭

Printed in Great Britain

09/13 (188088)